KT-584-229

LIGHT AND SOUND

Written by
Mike Clemmet

Illustrated by
Terry Kennett, Line & Line, Adrienne Salgado
and Salvatore Tomaselli

Edited by
Caroline White

Designed by
Clare Davey

Picture research by
Emma Segal

CONTENTS

The sense of sight

A long time ago people thought our eyes gave out rays that helped us to see. Nowadays we know that rays do not shine out of our eyes.

We are able to see because light comes into our eyes. If we did not need light to see, we would be able to see in the dark.

Light comes mainly from the sun. Even on a cloudy day we see by sunlight. The light hits the clouds and is scattered, but it still gets through.

At night the moon reflects light from the sun. When there is no moon, there may be a little starlight.

If we are indoors and it is dark, we can turn on a torch or a lamp. The light bounces off things in the room and comes into our eyes. This is how we see them.

In the Middle Ages people thought our eyes gave out rays of light.

Light comes from a source and bounces off things into our eyes.

A buzzard can see a small lizard or even a beetle on the ground while it is soaring high in the air.

The world around us

To survive we need to make sense of the world around us. We do this by using our five senses: taste, touch, smell, sight and hearing.

We mostly use the sense of sight to find out about our environment. Animals have a more highly developed sense of hearing and smell.

Did you know?

• Dogs do not see colours and their vision is blurred, but they can smell scents many times fainter than we can.

• Birds have a much keener sense of sight than humans.

Rays of light

We cannot see light. All we can see is the light source, such as a car headlight, and where the light lands. Scientists talk about light 'rays' to explain the behaviour of light.

Light rays travel in straight lines. Surveyors use this information to help them plan straight routes. They use an instrument called a theodolite to make sure roads are straight.

Surveyors use a theodolite to measure angles.

You can see light beams shining from car headlights or a torch. This is because the light is scattered by pollution and dirt particles in the air.

Pollution and dust particles are lit up in the beam from the torch.

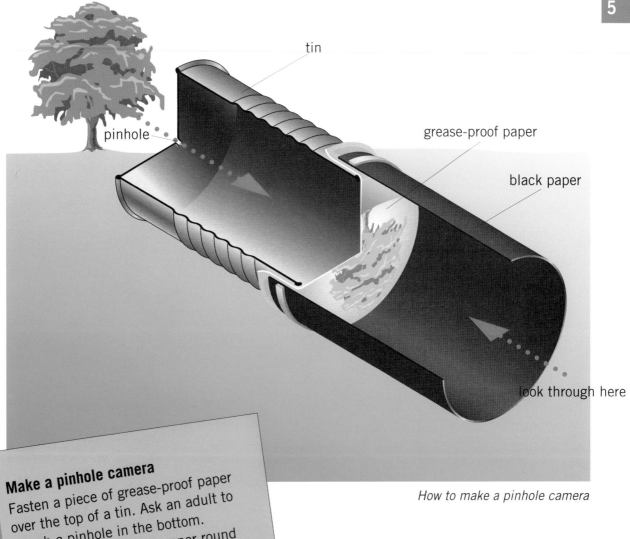

tin

pinhole

grease-proof paper

black paper

look through here

How to make a pinhole camera

Make a pinhole camera
Fasten a piece of grease-proof paper over the top of a tin. Ask an adult to punch a pinhole in the bottom. Fasten a piece of black paper round the top to cut out light from the side.

If you point a pinhole camera at a window, you will see a picture on the grease-proof paper. What do you notice about the picture? Can you think why it is like this? Pinhole cameras work because light travels in straight lines.

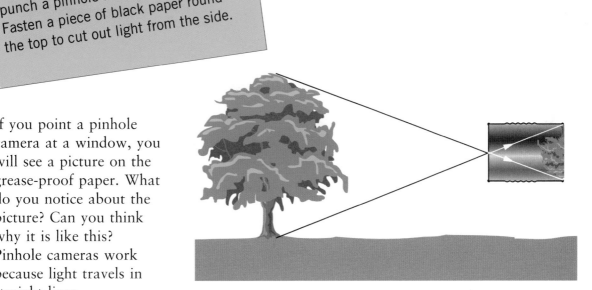

The rays cross over at the pinhole, so the picture looks upside down.

Shadows

If you go outside on a bright sunny day, you will see your shadow on the ground. Shadows are always cast on the side away from the sun.

Your body stops some of the light from the sun hitting the ground.

What is a shadow?

Light can pass through glass. Things that let light pass through them are called transparent. Our bodies will not let light pass through them. Things that absorb or reflect light are called opaque.

Rays of light come down in straight lines from the sun and make the ground around you bright. Your shadow is the bit of ground that does not get any light because your body is in the way.

Night and day

If you hold a ball up in sunlight, one side is bright and the other side is dark. This is because the ball is opaque. Light cannot pass through it, and only the side towards the sun is bright.

The Earth is like a giant ball. The side facing the sun is light. Here it is day. The other side of the Earth is in shadow. Here it is night. The Earth is continuously spinning and makes a complete turn in 24 hours. When one part moves into the shadow, night falls. When it moves out of the shadow, day breaks.

Journey through space

The sun is millions of miles away from Earth. To reach us, the light from the sun has to travel through empty space. Astronomers know that there are huge explosions taking place on the sun all the time. We never hear them because sound cannot travel through empty space.

If you put an electric buzzer in a bottle and suck out all the air, you cannot hear the buzzer because there is no air to carry the sound to you. You can still see the buzzer, because light can travel through empty space.

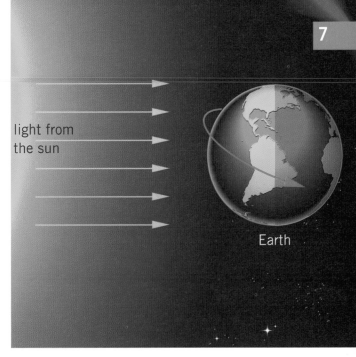

light from the sun

Earth

The side of the Earth facing the sun is in daylight. On the dark side, it is night.

On the moon

Astronauts on the moon cannot hear each other even if they shout and stand very close together. This is because there is no air on the moon and sound cannot travel through empty space. They could communicate by flashing lights because light can travel through a vacuum, where there is no air.

Astronauts on the moon cannot hear each other because there is no air for the sound to travel through.

Sources of light

We cannot see in the dark. Darkness is the absence of light. We need light to see. Things that give out light are called sources of light.

How far can you see?

If you look out to sea on a clear day, you can see as far as the horizon. This is about five miles away. You cannot see round the curve of the Earth because light travels in straight lines. If you stand higher up, you can see further.

The sun

This is not the furthest you can see. On a clear day you can see the sun. (You should never look directly at the sun because you could damage your eyes.) The sun is about 150 million kilometres away.

The stars

On a clear night you can see the stars. The nearest star is forty million million kilometres away. It is so far away that the light from it takes over four years to reach Earth. Some stars are so far away that their light takes thousands of millions of years to reach Earth. They are billions and billions of kilometres away and yet you can still see them.

How do you see stars? Stars shine and give out light. The light travels through space and enters your eyes. The sun is a star. It is just like the stars you see at night, but is so close to Earth that you can see it during the daytime. Because the sun is very bright, it stops you seeing the other stars.

The person on the clifftop can see further because he is higher up.

The moon

The moon does not give out light. We can see the moon because sunlight is reflected from it. You only see the part of the moon that is being hit by light from the sun. This is why the moon looks different at different times.

Most of the moon is lit up by the sun.

Only part of the moon is lit up by the sun.

moon

Earth's shadow

Earth

The first astronauts to land on the moon looked up and saw Earth. This was possible because the Earth was reflecting light from the sun, and some of it was going towards the moon.

The Earth casts a shadow just like any other solid object. Sometimes the moon, as it goes round the Earth, goes into the shadow. Because there is no light hitting the moon or being reflected, you cannot see it. This is called an eclipse.

In an eclipse, the moon is in the Earth's shadow and is not lit up by the sun's light.

Mirrors

When light hits something with a rough surface it is reflected in all directions. If light hits a smooth, flat surface all the rays are reflected at the same angle.

On a still day the surface of water is flat and smooth. Light rays from objects round a lake hit the surface of the water and are reflected at the same angle.

On a still day you see a perfect reflection in the water.

On a windy day you do not see a perfect reflection.

On a windy day, there are waves and ripples. The light hits the rough surface and is reflected in all directions.

Mirrors have smooth, flat, shiny surfaces. When a ray of light travels in a straight line and hits a mirror, it is reflected. If it hits the mirror at an angle, it is reflected at the same angle.

When you look at your own reflection in a mirror and move your right hand, it looks as though your reflection is moving its left hand. Reflections seem to be turned round from left to right.

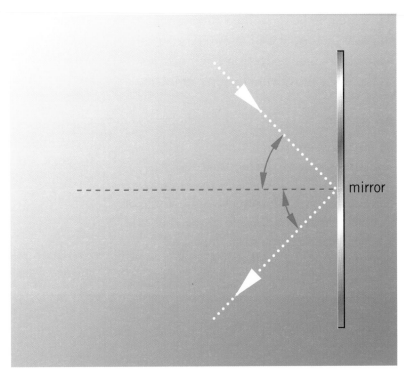

The ray of light is reflected away at the same angle as it hits the mirror.

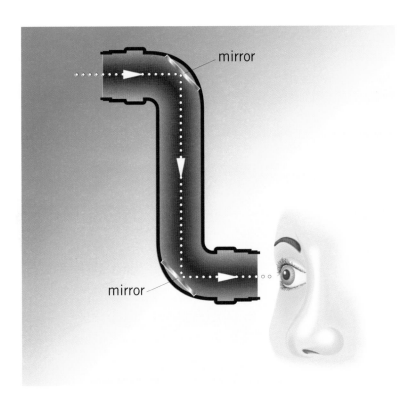

Periscopes use mirrors to let you see things that you could not otherwise see.

Periscopes

Mirrors can help you to see over the heads of people in crowds. Periscopes have two mirrors in them. You can often buy them at big parades. Light from the parade hits the top mirror and is reflected down the tube. It then hits the bottom mirror and is reflected into your eyes. You can now see over people's heads!

Submarines use periscopes so they can stay underwater and still see what is on the surface.

Echoes

Most people have walked through a subway or tunnel and shouted. You can hear your voice reflecting back off the walls. We call reflected sound an echo.

All at sea

Sound travels through water. Warships find submarines by sending out short bursts of sound. If there is a submarine below, some of the sound is reflected from it. The echoes travel back to the ship and are picked up by microphones. The equipment used is called ASDIC.

Fishing boats use echoes to find fish. They too send out pulses of sound. The sound is reflected off the shoals of fish and back to the ship. This tells the crew where to drop their nets.

Scientists can tell how deep the sea is by using an echo-sounder similar to ASDIC. It sends out sound that is reflected off the bottom of the sea and back to the ship.

The sound from the warship bounces off the submarine and back to the ship.

Oil prospecting

To find out if there is likely to be oil under the ground, oil companies have to look at the layers of rock beneath the Earth's crust. They do this by setting off an explosion. The sound travels through the rocks and is reflected off the different layers back up to microphones at the surface. A computer can then work out from the echoes how the layers of rock are arranged.

The sound from the explosion bounces off the layers of rock and back to the surface.

Animal echoes

Bats cannot see very well. They find their way around by sending out squeaks. The squeaks are reflected off objects around them. The bats pick up the echoes with their sensitive ears and work out where the objects are. This helps them to find their way in the dark and capture food.

Bats hunt by sending out sound and listening for the echoes.

high squeaks sent out by bat

echoes bouncing off insect

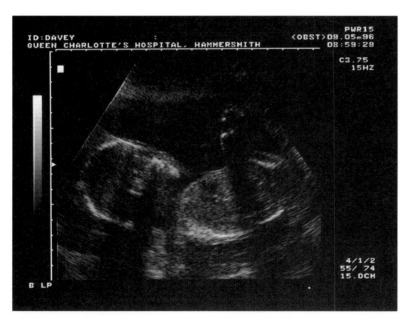

Ultrasound echoes were used to take this picture of a baby inside the mother.

Ultrasound

Doctors use ultrasound echoes to see babies before they are born. They send pulses of sound through the mother's body and pick up the echoes. A computer uses this information to build up a picture of the baby on screen. This helps doctors to detect any abnormalities. They can even tell whether it is a boy or a girl.

Did you know?

Scientists are developing an ASDIC system for blind people. A piece of equipment the size of a torch gives out very high sounds. The echoes are picked up by receivers in ear pieces. Because the sounds are too high for humans to hear, the ear pieces have special microphones that turn them into sounds within the human hearing range.

How far?

It is often important to know how far away things are. Animals that hunt need to know how far away their prey is. The prey needs to detect hunters so they can escape.

Different speeds

At a cricket match you see the ball hit the bat before you hear the sound. Why is this?

Light moves much faster than sound. In fact the speed of light is the fastest thing in the universe. Nothing can travel faster than light. You see the ball being hit before you hear the sound because it takes a lot less time for light to travel to your eyes than it does for sound to travel to your ears.

Light travels approximately a million times faster than sound. In a thunderstorm the light from the lightning reaches you almost straight away. The sound takes longer. You can tell how far away the flashes are if you count the seconds between the flash and the thunder and then times it by three.

Stereo vision

Human beings have two eyes. This is so we can work out how far away things are. The closer an object is, the greater the angle between the rays of light. Our brain uses this angle to work out how far away an object is. This is called stereo vision. It gives depth and clarity to what we see.

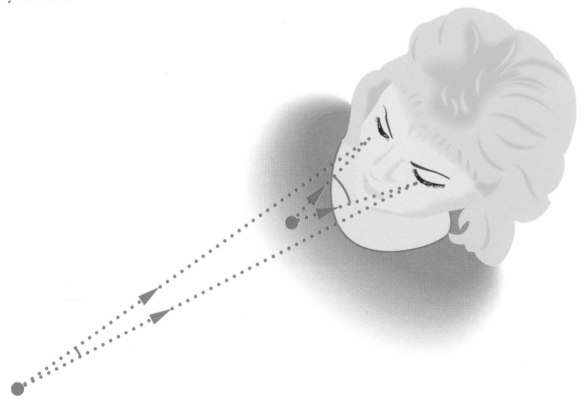

The closer an object is, the wider the angle between the rays of light coming from it.

Hunting

Rabbits have eyes at the sides of their heads. They can see almost all the way round themselves. This is important because they are hunted by foxes and need to be able to spot danger and run away. Rabbits do not hunt other animals.

A rabbit's eyes are set in the sides of its head.

Foxes hunt and need to be able to tell how far away their prey is. This is why they have eyes at the front of their heads. Animals that hunt need good stereo vision.

Rabbits have ears they can turn in all directions. This helps them to hear all around themselves. Hunting animals have ears that are more fixed and point forwards. They can use sound to work out how far away their prey is.

A fox has eyes set in the front of its head so it can judge the distance of its prey more easily.

Judging distance

Hold your elbows by your side and put your hands out in front of you. Hold a pencil in each hand with the points facing each other. Close one eye. Now move your hands together and make the points of the pencils meet exactly. Try it again with the other eye shut. Now try it with both eyes open. It is easier with both eyes open because you can judge distances more easily.

The speed of light

Light travels so fast that we often do not think of it as having a speed at all. When you turn on a lamp, the light seems to reach your eyes straight away. This is because light travels at three hundred thousand kilometres per second.

The sun is roughly ninety-three million miles away from the Earth. If you drove a car non-stop at a hundred miles an hour, it would take you over a hundred years to go that far. Light does it in just eight minutes.

The sun is our nearest star. The planets, including Earth, go round the sun. The closest that any other planet gets to us is Venus, at about forty million kilometres.

The furthest away that planets get from Earth is when they are on the other side of the sun. Pluto is furthest away from Earth. The greatest distance that it gets from us is about six thousand million kilometres. At this distance, the light from Pluto takes roughly five hours to reach us.

In the solar system the planets go round the sun in orbits that are nearly circular.

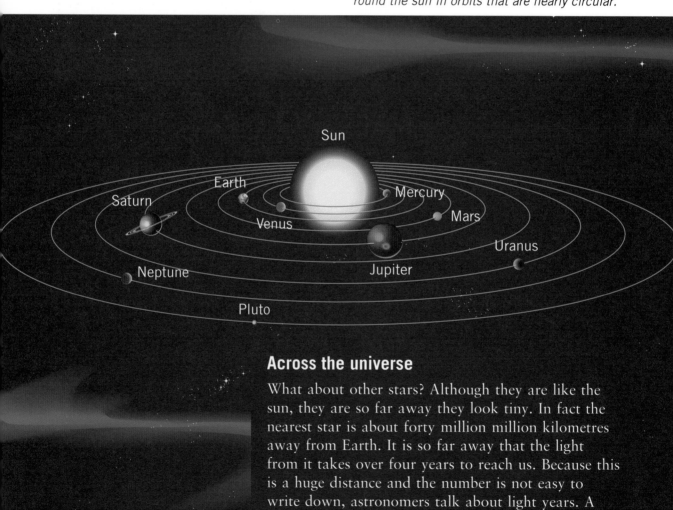

Across the universe

What about other stars? Although they are like the sun, they are so far away they look tiny. In fact the nearest star is about forty million million kilometres away from Earth. It is so far away that the light from it takes over four years to reach us. Because this is a huge distance and the number is not easy to write down, astronomers talk about light years. A light year is the distance that light travels in a year. It is roughly nine and a half million million kilometres. The nearest star is about four light years away.

When you look at the nearest star, you are seeing light that left it more than four years ago. Most stars are even further away than this. Some are thousands of millions of light years away. So when you look up at night you are seeing the stars as they used to be years ago.

If a star were to explode today, you would not see the explosion for years. In fact some of the stars that you see in the sky may not be there any longer, and we will not know about it until the last of their light reaches us.

Stars you see at night are so far away that light from them takes years to reach us.

This is the remains of a star that exploded millions of years ago.

The speed of sound

The first aeroplane to carry a human was built by George Cayley one hundred and fifty years ago. It was a glider and had no engine. People still fly in gliders for sport today. Gliders depend on air currents to keep them up.

This is a glider and has no engine.

Wilbur and Orville Wright made the first flight in an aeroplane with an engine.

About ninety years ago, two brothers called Wilbur and Orville Wright put an engine in a glider. They made the first powered flight at Kitty Hawk in the USA. The flight lasted approximately one minute and covered about three hundred metres.

After this, aeroplane design improved and people were able to fly further and faster. In 1909 Louis Bleriot made the first flight across the English Channel – about forty kilometres. Eighteen years later, Charles Lindbergh flew non-stop across the Atlantic – several thousand kilometres.

Over the next few years, aeroplanes got faster and faster. In the Second World War, fighter planes were able to fly at several hundred kilometres an hour. They had engines that turned a propeller to move them through the air.

During the war, the first jet engines were put in planes. Jet planes were able to go a lot faster than those driven by a propeller.

The sound barrier

There seemed to be a barrier to the speed of the jet planes. Nothing was able to fly faster than the speed of sound – 1180 kilometres an hour.

Then, in 1947, a plane with a rocket engine broke the sound barrier. The speed of sound is called Mach 1, after an Austrian scientist, Ernst Mach. In 1970 Concorde crossed the Atlantic for the first time at Mach 2 – twice the speed of sound.

The Spitfire was one of the fastest planes in World War II. Its engine turned a propeller.

Concorde has jet engines.

Changing speed

The speed of sound is not fixed; it depends what it is travelling through. Sound travels at a slightly different speed through cold air than hot air. It travels at slightly different speeds through wet air and dry air. It travels faster through water than air. In fact the 'stiffer' the material, the faster sound travels through it.

Light is different. It travels fastest through a vacuum, where there is no air. It travels a little more slowly through air and slower still through glass.

Curved mirrors

Sometimes there is a Hall of Mirrors at the fairground. When you look at your reflection in the mirrors, it is distorted and makes you look odd. This is because the mirrors are curved.

Curved mirrors twist your reflection.

Going in

You can get a similar effect if you look at your reflection in a shiny spoon. Look at the side of a spoon that bends inwards. Surfaces like this are called concave (you can remember this word because it has 'cave' in it – and caves go inwards). Your reflection will be upside down.

Now get a dress-making pin. Hold the spoon in one hand and the pin in the other, about 12 cm away from the spoon. As you move the pin towards the concave surface of the spoon, a funny thing happens. The reflection gets bigger, until it appears bigger than the pin. We say it is magnified. If you keep on moving the pin closer to the spoon, the reflection turns the right way up and is still magnified.

If you go into a chemist's shop, you may find shaving mirrors for sale. Shaving mirrors are concave. Look at your reflection when you are standing quite close to one. You will see that it is magnified. Now look in the mirror from a distance. Your reflection is upside down, just like in the spoon.

Concave mirrors are also used in telescopes to look at the stars and planets. They give a magnified reflection.

Telescopes for looking at the stars use concave mirrors.

Shaving mirrors

Face a window in a room and hold a sheet of white paper in one hand and a shaving mirror in the other. Shine the reflected light from the window onto the paper. Move the mirror towards and away from the paper. You should be able to focus an image of the window onto it. Can you do this with a flat mirror?

Going out

The other side of the spoon bends outwards. It is called convex. Try the same experiment with a pin. You will see that the reflection is always the right way up and small. Convex mirrors are used as driving mirrors because they give a wider reflection than flat mirrors.

Driving mirrors are convex and give the driver a wider picture.

Bending light

The path followed by light bends when it passes from air into water. Light rays bend whenever they go from one material into another.

Fill a sink with water and put a coin at the bottom on the side furthest away from you. Put your head down until you can just see the coin over the rim of the sink. Now pull out the plug. Keep your head still and look at the coin.

Change of direction

As the water runs out of the sink the coin appears to sink, until you can no longer see it. This happens because light bends as it goes from water into air. This bending of light is called refraction.

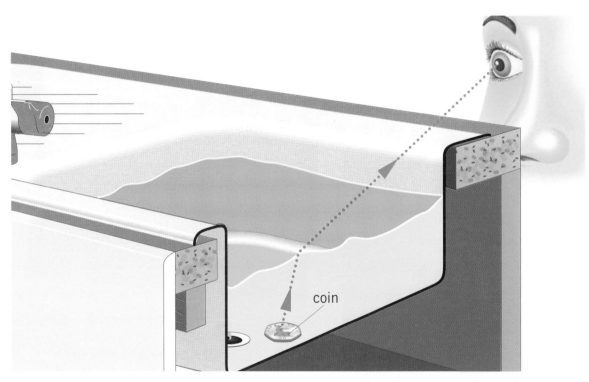

coin

Light from the coin bends as it goes from the water into the air.

It means you can see the coin when it is covered by water, but not when the sink is empty. This is why you should always check the depth of water before you step into it – refraction makes it look more shallow than it really is.

The water on the horizon is not really there: it is a mirage.

Light is refracted when it goes from water into air (and from air into water) because water is denser than air. Similarly, light bends when it goes from hot air into cold air, because hot air is less dense than cold air. If you drive down a road on a very hot day, you sometimes see 'water' on the horizon. When you get close to the 'water' it disappears. This is because you are not really seeing water. Light from the blue sky is being refracted by hot air into your eyes, and it looks like water.

In deserts this often happens because the air near the ground is very hot. People see mirages of things that are over the horizon.

Prisms

Light bends (is refracted) when it goes into and out of glass. You do not notice this at a window because the glass is flat and even. A triangular piece of glass or plastic is called a prism. When a ray of light hits a triangular prism it bends.

The light bends as it goes into and comes out of the prism.

Lenses

If you put two triangular prisms together with their bases touching and shine light through them, the rays will bend.

If the rays of light are parallel before they go into the glass, they will be bent towards each other when they come out.

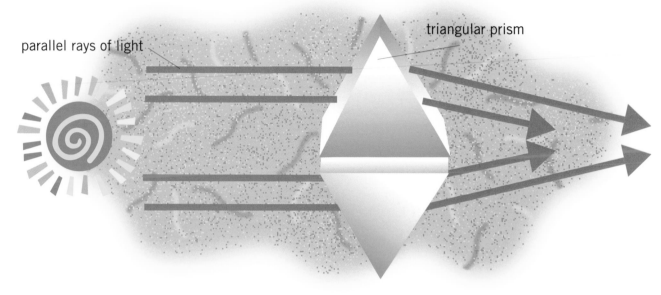

parallel rays of light

triangular prism

The rays of light meet and cross over when they come out of the prisms.

Convex lens

A convex lens is like two prisms stuck together, except the faces are curved. The curving is carefully worked out so that parallel rays of light are bent at just the right angle to all meet at a point.

We say the rays are focused. The point where they meet is called the focal point of the lens. The only ray of light that is not bent is the one that goes exactly through the centre of the lens.

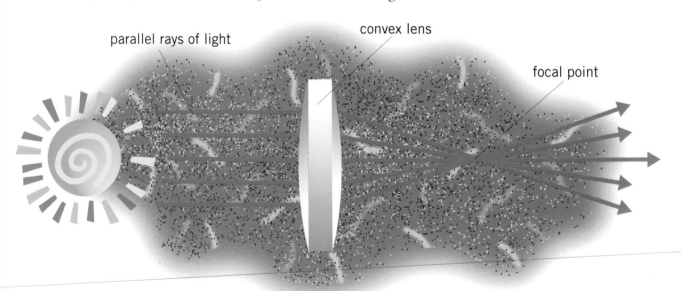

parallel rays of light

convex lens

focal point

A convex lens focuses rays of light to a focal point.

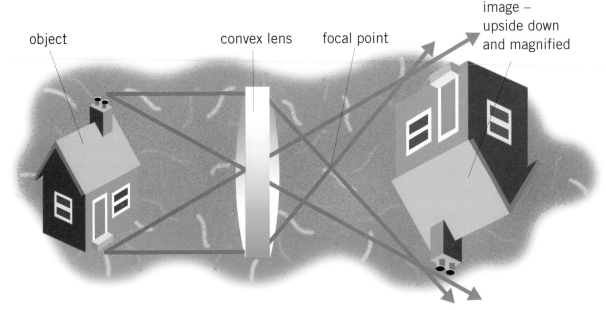

object   convex lens   focal point   image – upside down and magnified

This is how a magnifying glass works.

If you look at an object through a convex lens, the rays of light look as if they are coming in straight lines from a larger object. You see a magnified image. What you actually see depends on how far away the object is from the lens.

Concave lens

A convex lens is like two prisms stuck base to base. You get a different effect if you use a concave lens. This time the rays of light are bent away from each other. We say they diverge, or get further apart. Concave lenses tend to make things look smaller.

Magnifying lens
What sort of lens does a magnifying glass have?

Move a magnifying glass towards and away from a piece of writing and see what sort of image you get at different distances.

A concave lens makes the rays of light spread apart and not come to a focal point.

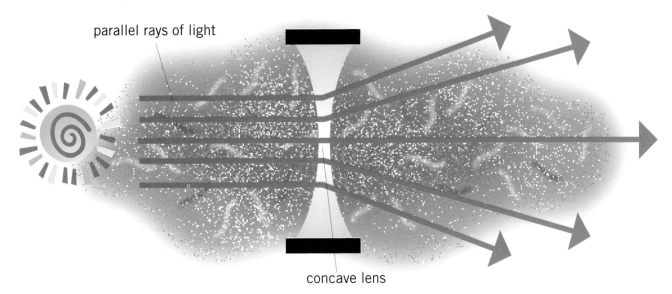

parallel rays of light

concave lens

Photographs

Convex lenses make light rays focus to a point. Because of this, you can use a convex lens to focus a picture onto a screen. This is what happens with a cinema projector or a slide projector.

If you coat paper with a substance that is affected by light and then shine light on it, the paper goes dark. If you put the paper at the back of a box which has a hole at the front and a lens inside, the lens focuses a picture onto the paper. The paper goes dark where the bright parts of the picture hit it. This is how a camera works.

The film in the camera goes darkest where the brightest light hits it. You get a picture where the lightest parts of the scene are dark and the darkest parts are light. This is called a negative.

If you shine light through a negative onto the same sort of paper, the same thing happens. You get a negative of the negative. The light parts of the scene look the right brightness.

The lights and darks are the wrong way round on the negative.

The lights and darks are the right way round on the finished photograph.

Early cameras were bulky and awkward to use.

A sharp picture

A camera lens cannot focus the whole picture. To get the part that you want in focus, you have to move the lens forwards or backwards until you get a clear image.

Exposure

The longer the light shines on the film, the darker the film gets. Early cameras had a shutter in front of the lens. The photographer would lift off the shutter and then put it back when the photograph was thought to have been exposed to enough light.

In those days films took a long time to react to the light: they were slow. Today, scientists have invented films that react very quickly to light and only need to be exposed for part of a second. Modern cameras have mechanical shutters that expose the film for just the right length of time. A lot of modern cameras have a light sensor in them that works out how light the scene is and automatically opens the shutter for the right amount of time.

The eye

The way our eyes work is a lot like a camera. At the back of the eye is a layer of cells called the retina. Its job is similar to that of the film in the camera: it is sensitive to light. When light hits the retina, messages are sent to the brain.

The optic nerve carries the messages to the brain. Where the optic nerve joins the eye there is a spot that is not sensitive to light. This is called the blind spot.

The parts of the eye

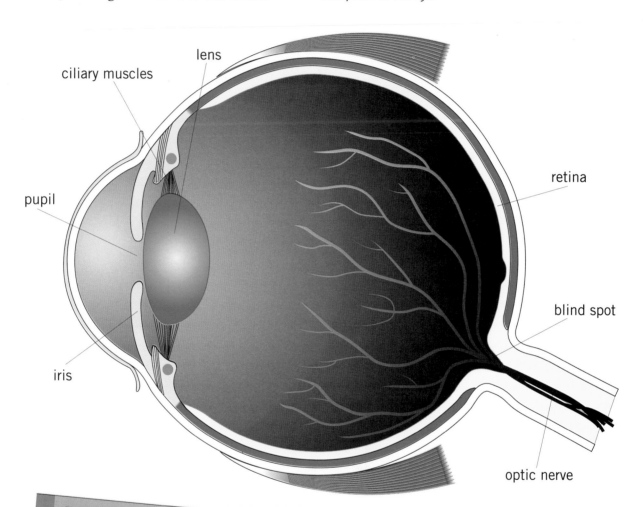

ciliary muscles

lens

pupil

iris

retina

blind spot

optic nerve

Blind spot

Draw a cross and a dot about 8 cm apart in a notebook and hold the book at arm's length. Close your left eye and stare at the cross with your right eye. Bring the book slowly towards you. At some point the dot will 'disappear'. This is because the light from the dot is falling on the blind spot in your right eye.

There is a lens in your eye that focuses the picture onto the retina. In a camera you focus different parts of the scene by moving the lens backwards and forwards. In your eye the lens can change shape. There are little muscles all round it called ciliary muscles. They contract to make the lens thinner to focus on things that are far away. They relax to make the lens fatter to focus on things that are close up.

The coloured part of your eye is called the iris. In the middle of the iris is a black circle called the pupil. This is the hole that lets light into your eye. In very bright light the pupil gets smaller so less light gets in and you are not blinded by the glare. When it is darker, the pupil gets bigger to let in more light.

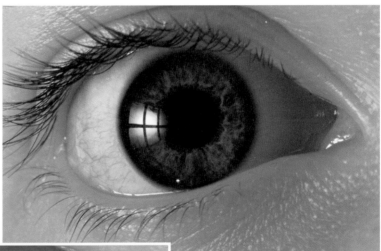

The pupil is small in bright light.

The eyeball is covered by a tough skin called the sclerotic coating. This is seen as the white of the eye. The sclerotic coating protects your eye from damage.

The pupil opens up in dim light.

Did you know?
Your eyeball is not empty. It is full of a kind of jelly that makes it keep its shape.

Recording sound

All sounds are made by something vibrating. The vibrations can be recorded and turned back into sound.

Alexander Bell

On 10 March 1876 the first ever telephone message was sent. Alexander Graham Bell was in one room of a house in Boston, USA. He spilt some acid and shouted into the mouthpiece, 'Mr Watson, come here – I want to see you!' In another room, his assistant heard the message.

When a drum skin vibrates, the sound spreads out in all directions.

The telephone was invented by Bell. As a boy he was interested in sound. He knew sound was caused by vibrations.

Think of a guitar. When you pluck the strings, they vibrate backwards and forwards. This is what makes the sound. When you bang a drum, the skin of the drum vibrates. As it vibrates, it makes the air particles near it vibrate. As these particles vibrate, they make the ones next to them vibrate. The vibrations spread through the air, getting more spread out and weaker as they travel away from the drum. In your throat you have vocal chords that vibrate and produce sound.

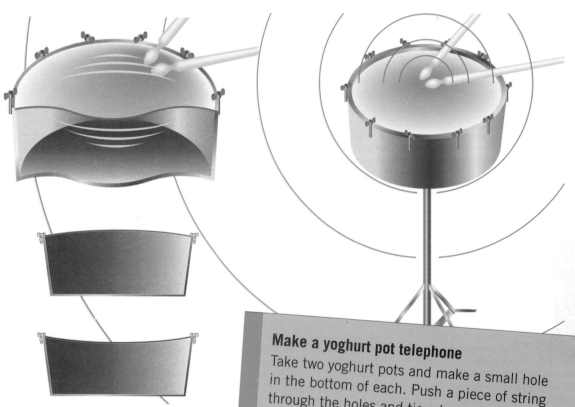

Make a yoghurt pot telephone

Take two yoghurt pots and make a small hole in the bottom of each. Push a piece of string through the holes and tie a knot at each end. Get someone else to hold one of the pots and pull the string tight between you. One person holds the pot to their ear and the other holds the pot to their mouth and speaks. The vibrations travel along the string to the other person's ear.

Bell was able to build a mouthpiece that turned the air vibrations into electrical vibrations in a wire.

He then built a receiver that took the electrical vibrations from the wire and made a thin piece of metal vibrate to reproduce the sounds from the mouthpiece. Microphones and loudspeakers today work in much the same way.

The first telephone was invented by Alexander Bell.

The needle on the arm of a record player vibrates as the grooves run past it.

Records

Look at a record through a magnifying glass. You will see lots of wavy grooves.

As the needle on the pick-up arm runs along the groove in the record, it vibrates because of the waviness. The vibrations are changed to electrical vibrations that make the diaphragm in the loudspeaker vibrate and produce sound.

The ear

Ears work in a similar way to a telephone mouthpiece or a microphone. The outer ear (the bit you can see on the side of your head) is like a funnel. It channels the vibrations of the air into the middle ear.

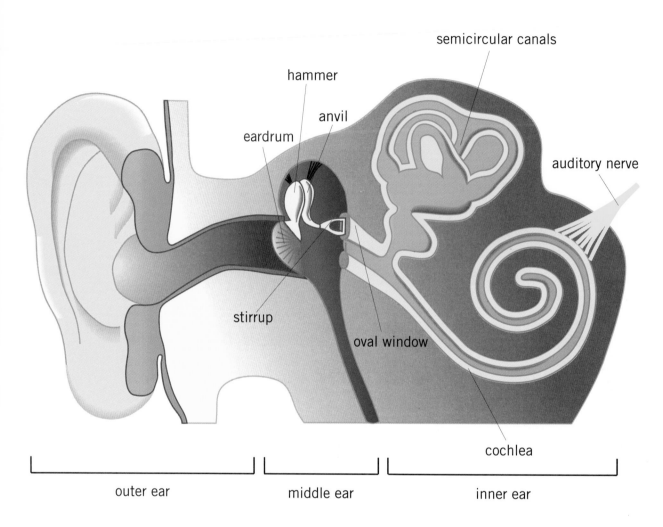

The parts of the ear

The middle ear

The vibrations hit the eardrum and make it vibrate. The eardrum is connected to three little bones called the hammer, anvil and stirrup. They are called this because of their shape. The hammer bone is connected to the eardrum. As the eardrum vibrates, it makes the hammer vibrate.

Because the three bones are connected, they all start to vibrate. The third tiny bone, the stirrup, is connected to a thin skin that covers the oval window at the entrance to the inner ear. When the bones vibrate, so does the skin.

The inner ear

In the inner ear there is a sheet of very thin skin called the oval window, stretched over an opening. The bones pass the sound vibrations along to this membrane.

The vibrations then pass into a fluid-filled tube called the cochlea. The cochlea is lined with tiny hairs that contain nerve endings. As the vibrations move the hairs, electrical impulses are set up that travel to the brain along the auditory nerve. The brain interprets the messages and we hear the sounds.

People who use noisy machinery have to wear ear protectors.

A sense of balance

Ears are not only for hearing. If you look at the diagram, you will see three semicirles that are at right angles to each other and point in different directions. These are called the semicircular canals and they help you to know what your position is.

Semicircular canals

The semicircular canals also help you to keep your balance. When you move your head, the liquid in the inner ear moves. These movements are picked up by nerve cells in the semicircular canals and produce messages that go to your brain. If this part of the ear is damaged by accident or illness, you feel sick and dizzy and lose your sense of balance.

It is not only disease that can damage your ears. Sounds that are too loud can make your ears vibrate too much. This damages the delicate bones, skin and nerve endings and you can become partly deaf. This is why people who use noisy machinery wear ear protectors.

Loudness and pitch

Everyone has a different voice. Some people can imitate other people's voices. If they are very good at it, they can make a living on the stage or television.

Most people have distinctive voices. Even in a crowded room you can probably pick out the voice of a friend or parent.

Animals also make distinctive sounds. A mother sheep can tell the bleating of her own lamb from all the others in the field.

What makes voices distinctive? One thing is how high or low the voice is. We call this pitch.

Some people have high-pitched voices and some have low-pitched ones. When you speak, you change the pitch of your voice all the time.

What is pitch?

Sound is produced by vibrations. When you speak, your vocal chords vibrate. This makes the air vibrate. The sound spreads out through the air as areas of high and low pressure. If the vibrations are fast, the areas of high pressure will be close together. If the vibrations are slow, they will be further apart.

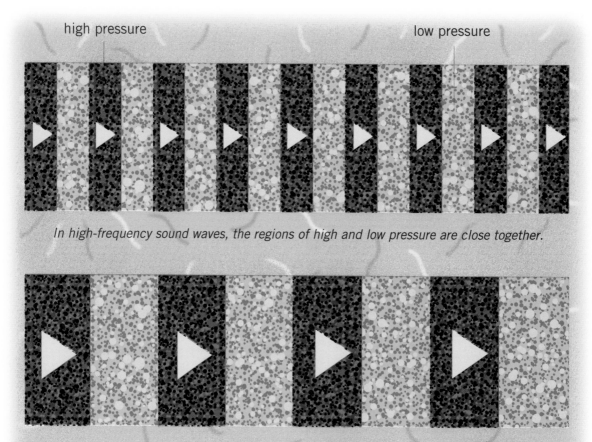

high pressure   low pressure

In high-frequency sound waves, the regions of high and low pressure are close together.

In low-frequency sound waves, the regions of high and low pressure are further apart.

We call these areas of high and low pressure sound waves. The high pressure areas are the peaks of the waves, and the low pressure areas are the troughs. The faster the vibrations, the more peaks there are per second – the peaks are produced more frequently.

The number of peaks per second is called the frequency of the sound wave. The greater the frequency, the higher the pitch. In other words, the faster the vibration, the higher the pitch of the sound.

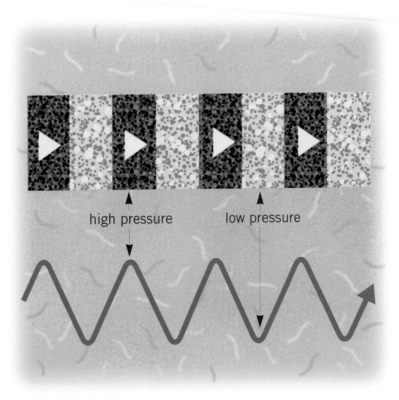

A sound wave is made up of areas of high and low pressure.

The louder the sound, the bigger the vibrations. The difference between the highest and lowest pressures is called the amplitude of the wave.

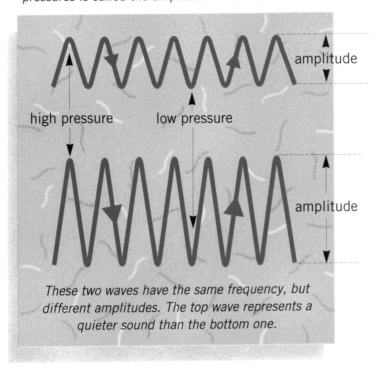

These two waves have the same frequency, but different amplitudes. The top wave represents a quieter sound than the bottom one.

Loudness

Another thing that makes our voices distinctive is how loud they are. The bigger the movements of your vocal chords, the louder the noise. We call the size of the vibrations the amplitude. The greater the amplitude, the louder the sound.

When we speak, we change the pitch and amplitude of our voice in a way that is typical of us. Impersonators can imitate this.

Musical sounds

Even if you do not know much about music, you can probably tell the sound of a guitar from the sound of a trumpet or clarinet. Different instruments produce different sounds.

All things that make a sound make the air shake back and forth very fast. These shaking movements are called vibrations. If the vibrations reach our ears, we hear the sound.

Strings

Different instruments make sounds in different ways. They are grouped together according to how they make sounds. One group has strings and includes the guitar. The player plucks the strings to make them vibrate.

Violins have strings too, but they are not plucked. The player runs the bow over them to make them vibrate.

How do you change the note?

- The shorter the string, the faster it vibrates. Players use their fingers to change the length of the strings.

- The tighter the string, the higher the note. There are screws to tighten and loosen the strings.

- The thicker the string, the lower the pitch. Different strings have different thicknesses.

The strings on a violin vibrate to make sounds.

Making different sounds
Take a piece of string and fasten one end to a table leg. Pull the string tight and pluck it. Let it go a bit slack and pluck it again. Pull it tight, pluck it, and then run your finger along it. Try doing the same thing with different thicknesses of string. What happens if you use wire?

The instruments in the woodwind section of an orchestra are blown to make vibrations.

Wind instruments

In trumpets, trombones and other brass instruments the player's lips vibrate to make the air in the instrument vibrate. The longer the instrument, the lower the note.

Brass instruments are long tubes full of air. They are 'curled up' to make them easier to play.

Clarinets, bassoons and other woodwind instruments have a reed in the mouthpiece. The player blows over the reed to make it vibrate.

Drums and gongs

Another part of the orchestra is the percussion section. This is made up of instruments that are struck to make them vibrate.

In the percussion section of an orchestra, the instruments are struck to make vibrations.

Changing the pitch
Take a glass jar and a stick. Hit the glass gently and listen to the sound. Pour some water into the jar. Strike it again. The sound will be higher. The pitch of the sound depends on the length of the column of air.

The rainbow

About three hundred years ago a scientist called Isaac Newton discovered that the light from the sun can be split up into light of different colours.

The story goes that while Isaac Newton was working in his room one day, he made a small hole in the blind to let in a ray of sunlight. He then held a triangular prism in the path of the light. The light went through the prism and onto a screen.

White light is split up by raindrops to make a rainbow.

Isaac Newton held a prism in the path of a beam of sunlight.

The light from the sun is called white light because it appears to be white. The light going into the prism was white light. The light shining onto the screen was coloured. The white light had been split up by the prism into red, orange, yellow, green, blue, indigo and violet light. These seven colours make up white light and are called the spectrum.

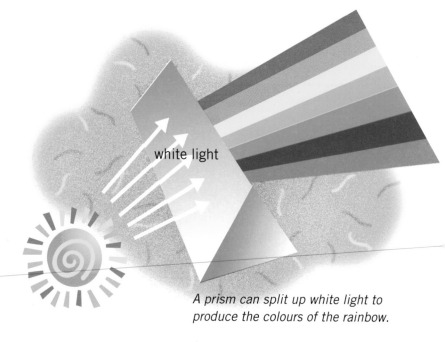

white light

A prism can split up white light to produce the colours of the rainbow.

Waves

The distance between the peaks of the light waves is called the wavelength. The number of peaks per second is called the frequency.

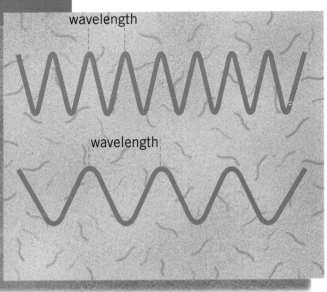

These two waves have different wavelengths. The peaks of the waves are different distances apart.

The same thing happens when white light goes through raindrops. This is why you sometimes see a rainbow when the sun shines during showers. The colours of the rainbow are the colours of the spectrum.

Did you know?
You can remember the order of the colours in the spectrum if you remember the saying: 'Richard Of York Gave Battle In Vain'. Each word starts with the same letter as one of the colours.

Light waves have a very, very high frequency - much higher than sound waves.

Just as different notes have different frequencies, different coloured light has different frequencies. The different colours are bent (refracted) by different amounts as they go through the prism.

Impaired vision

Not everybody has perfect eyesight. There are several ways in which eyesight can be impaired. It can usually be corrected by wearing glasses.

Colour blindness

The wires in electric plugs are colour coded. The live wire used to be red and the earth wire used to be green. Nowadays the live wire is brown and the earth wire is green-and-yellow stripes. The colours were changed because approximately one in every twelve males is colour blind. This does not mean they cannot see colours at all. It means they get colours mixed up. The most common sort is red-green colour blindness, where people cannot tell the difference between red and green.

Short sight

People who are short-sighted can only see a short distance clearly. This is because the lens in their eye focuses light short of the retina. They can see clearly when they are given glasses with a concave lens. The lens causes the rays of light to diverge before they hit the eye. This makes the light focus further back onto the retina.

This is how the picture above might look to a person who is red-green colour blind.

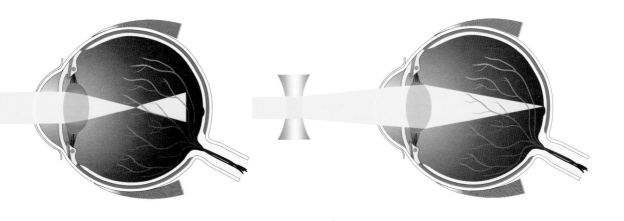

Short sight: the rays focus in front of the retina.

Concave lenses correct short sight.

Long sight

Some people are long-sighted. They can see things clearly if they are a long way away, but they cannot see things that are close to them. This is because the lens in their eye does not focus the light exactly onto the retina.

People with long sight wear glasses with convex lenses. A convex lens makes the rays of light converge before they hit the eye and focus the light onto the retina.

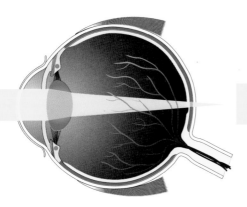

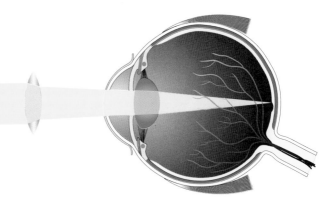

Long sight: the rays focus behind the retina.

Convex lenses correct long sight.

Mixing colours

White light is made up of the different colours of the spectrum: red, orange, yellow, green, blue, indigo and violet. When white light shines onto a white object, all the colours are reflected. This is why it looks white.

When white light shines onto a blue object, only the blue light is reflected. The rest of the colours are absorbed. This is why it looks blue.

The retina is covered in tiny cones that are sensitive to coloured light. They send messages to the brain to say which colour light is hitting them.

Mixing light

All the colours in white light can be made by mixing red, green and blue. We call these primary colours. There are three sorts of cones on your retina. Each is sensitive to a different primary colour.

When you look at the light from a red object, only the red-sensitive cones react. If you look at the light from a yellow object, the red and green cones react. The messages go to your brain and it works out how much of each colour there is, and you see the object as yellow. A mixture of red and green light makes yellow!

Mixing paint

When you are painting, you cannot mix yellow. In paints, yellow is a primary colour and green is not. Green can be made by mixing blue and yellow.

It is not possible to make paints that reflect pure colours. Blue paint reflects blue light and some green light; it absorbs all the other colours. Yellow paint reflects red and green light; it absorbs everything else. A mixture of blue and yellow paint absorbs every colour except green – so it looks green.

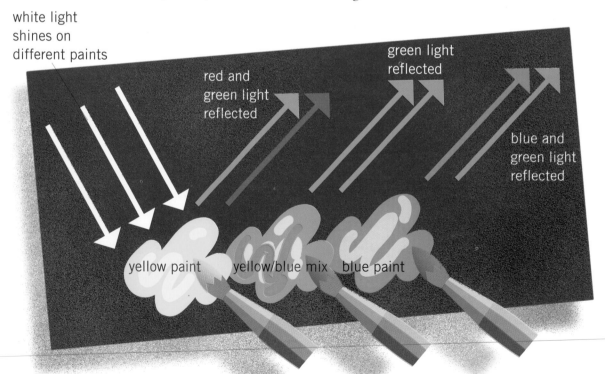

white light shines on different paints

red and green light reflected

green light reflected

blue and green light reflected

yellow paint   yellow/blue mix   blue paint

Yellow paint reflects red and green light and absorbs all the other colours.

Television

The screen of a colour television gives out three colours. Your brain mixes these colours to make the hundreds or thousands of different colours that you see in the picture.

Film

Colour film is the same. One chemical in the film is affected by red light, one by green light and one by blue light. These three colours are mixed together to give you all the other colours.

This photo shows just the blues.

This photo shows just the reds.

This photo shows all the colours put together.

This photo shows just the greens.

Radiation

It is not just light that we get from the sun. We also get heat. Although we cannot see the heat, we can feel it.

A wider spectrum

When you go outside on a sunny day, the sunshine feels hot on your skin. White skin will go red from the effect of the sunlight if you stay out in it for too long.

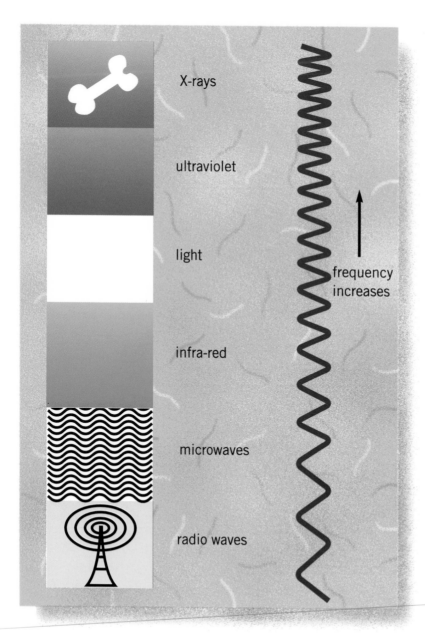

It is not just heat that affects skin. There is something else that we get from the sun – ultraviolet rays. Heat, light and ultraviolet are all radiated from the sun. Radiation from the sun is called electromagnetic radiation.

Heat and ultraviolet, like light, are made up of waves. The waves in heat are further apart than light waves. We say their wavelength is longer. The waves in ultraviolet are closer together than light waves. We say their wavelength is shorter.

White light can be split up into different colours called the spectrum. Radiation from the sun can be split up into a spectrum that is wider than just coloured light. It contains the light we can see (visible light) and heat, as well as other sorts of radiation such as ultraviolet, microwaves, X-rays and radio waves.

Heat is sometimes known as infra-red radiation. 'Infra' means 'below'. Infra-red, or heat, is below red in the spectrum. 'Ultra' means 'above'. Ultraviolet is above violet in the spectrum.

X-rays

ultraviolet

light

frequency increases

infra-red

microwaves

radio waves

The electromagnetic spectrum

Too much sunlight can be harmful to white skin.

Too much ultraviolet

Too much ultraviolet radiation is harmful. It can cause eye complaints and skin cancer. Air stops some of the ultraviolet from the sun reaching the Earth's surface.

If you go up a high mountain, there is less air above you so more ultraviolet hits you. Fortunately there is a gas high up in the atmosphere that cuts out a lot of the ultraviolet. The gas is called ozone.

Ozone holes

We have released a lot of chemicals into the air that are destroying the ozone layer. It means more ultraviolet now reaches the Earth's surface. This is why you should never stay out in the sunlight too long. If you do go sunbathing, wear suntan cream that absorbs ultraviolet and stops it affecting your skin. Sunglasses will stop the ultraviolet affecting your eyes.

Moving pictures

The first moving pictures were shown about a hundred years ago. They were black and white, silent and lasted about five or ten minutes.

Look out of the window for a while and then quickly close your eyes. You should find that even with your eyes shut you still 'see' a picture. This is called persistence of vision. It happens because the retina keeps on sending signals to your brain for a short while after light has stopped falling on it.

Make a bird in a cage

Cut a 4 cm x 4 cm square out of card. Make two small holes about 1 cm apart on opposite sides of the square. Thread a piece of string through the holes and tie the ends together to make a loop. Draw a bird on one side of the square and a cage on the other. Hold one end of the loop in each hand. Twist up the loop, then pull so that the card spins quickly. You should see the bird in the cage.

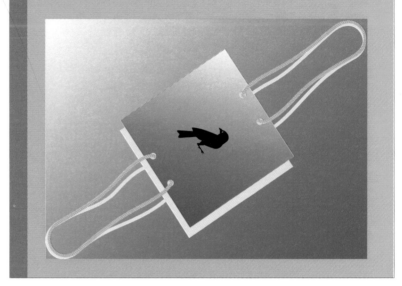

Cinema uses persistence of vision. Cameras have a reel of film running through them. The shutter opens 25 times per second and takes one still picture after another. The film is then developed.

To show the film, you put it into a projector. The pictures are shone one after the other onto a screen. You see 25 pictures each second. Because of persistence of vision you are still 'seeing' the last picture when the next one is shown. The result is that you see a smooth picture of the action.

A moving picture is made up of lots of still pictures.

Changing speed

In the early days of cinema, fewer pictures were taken per second. When these old films are shown using a modern projector, the action looks speeded up and jerky.

Slow-motion film is made by taking hundreds of pictures a second and then showing them at 25 pictures per second.

If you take one picture of a growing plant every hour, and then show it at 25 pictures per second, you see the growth speeded up.

Television

A picture is built up on a television screen by firing a beam of tiny particles at it to make a spot of light. There are three different sorts of materials on the screen. Each makes a red, green or blue spot when the beam hits it. The beam can be changed to make the light brighter and dimmer. The spot is made to scan backwards and forwards over the screen to build up a picture. Lots of new pictures are built up every second, so that you see smooth movement.

The beam builds up a picture on the televsion screen.

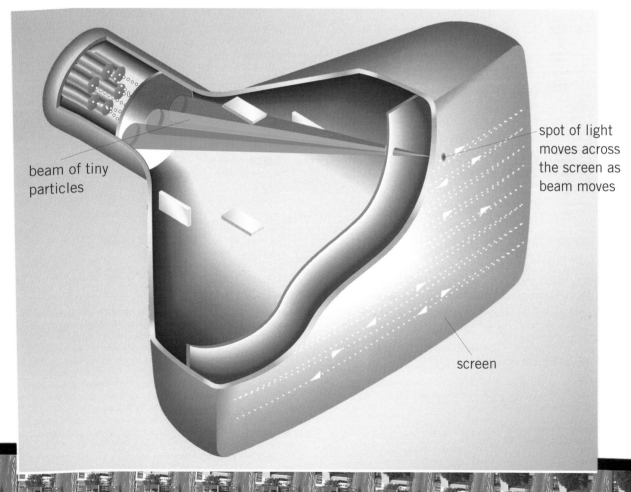

beam of tiny particles

spot of light moves across the screen as beam moves

screen

5

Published by BBC Educational Publishing, a division of BBC Education, BBC White City, 201 Wood Lane, London W12 7TS
First published 1996
© Mike Clemmet/BBC Worldwide (through BBC Education) 1996
The moral right of the author has been asserted.

Paperback: 0 563 37505 1
Hardback: 0 563 37557 4

Colour reproduction by Dot Gradations, England
Cover origination by Sonicon Ltd, England
Printed and bound by Cambus Litho Ltd, Scotland

Illustrations: © Terry Kennett 1996 (pages 23, 24, 25, 34, 35, 38, 39, 42 and 44), © Line & Line 1996 (pages 5, 7, 9, 11, 12, 13, 14, 16, 22, 30, 46 and 47), © Adrienne Salgado 1996 (pages 2, 6, 7, 8 and 38), © Salvatore Tomaselli 1996 (pages 28, 32, 33 and 41)

Photo credits: BBC/Luke Finn pp. 4 (bottom), 31 (bottom); BBC/Simon Pugh pp. 40 (both), 43 (all); Britstock-IFA/Diaf p. 18 (top); Britstock-IFA/TPL p. 19 (bottom); Bruce Coleman Collection/Jane Burton p. 15 (top); Bruce Coleman Collection/Christer Fredriksson pp. 38-39; Kindly provided by Clare Davey pp. 13, 46-47; Ecoscene/Nick Hawkes p. 10 (bottom); Robert Harding Picture Library/Roy Rainford p.10 (top); Hulton Getty p. 27; Incredible, Fantastic Old Toy Show, Lincoln/D. Overton p. 20; The Mansell Collection pp. 18 (bottom), 31 (top); David Noble Photography p. 9 (top and bottom); Courtesy of Ordnance Survey/Alan Brindle p. 4 (top); Performing Arts Library/Clive Barda p. 37 (bottom); Quadrant Picture Library/Autoexpress p. 21 (bottom); Rex Features London p. 19 (top); Rex Features London/Clive Dixon p. 33; Rex Features London/Nils Jorgensen p. 15 (bottom); The Royal Society for the Protection of Birds Photolibrary/Mark Hamblin p. 3; Keith Saunders/LSO p. 37 (top); Science Photo Library/Adam Hart-Davis p. 29 (top and bottom); Science Photo Library/NOAO p. 17 (bottom); Science Photo Library/Roger Ressmeyer p. 21 (top); Science Photo Library/John Sanford p. 17 (top); Emma Segal p. 26 (left and right); Zefa Pictures UK pp. 23, 36, 45

Front cover: Ace Photo Agency/P. & M. Walton (main); Redferns Music Picture Library/David Redfern (inset)